# DEDICATED TO
# THE ONES I LOVE

### Edited by Andrew Head

# DEDICATED TO
# THE ONES I LOVE

# EDITED BY ANDREW HEAD

First published in Great Britain in 1997 by

1-2 Wainman Road, Woodston,
Peterborough, PE2 7BU
Telephone  (01733) 230746
Fax (01733) 230751

HB ISBN 1 86188 701 9
SB ISBN 1 86188 706 X

# Foreword

Although we are a nation of poetry writers we are accused of not reading poetry and not buying poetry books: after many years of listening to the incessant gripes of poetry publishers, I can only assume that the books they publish, in general, are books that most people do not want to read. Poetry should not be obscure, introverted, and as cryptic as a crossword puzzle: it is the poet's duty to reach out and embrace the world.

The world owes the poet nothing and we should not be expected to dig and delve into a rambling discourse searching for some inner meaning.

The reason we write poetry (and almost all of us do) is because we want to communicate: an ideal; an idea; or a specific feeling. Poetry is as essential in communication, as a letter; a radio; a telephone, and the main criteria for selecting the poems in this anthology is very simple: they communicate.

Our family are the people who care for us and love us unconditionally. They are always there, through the good times and bad, providing their support when we need it the most. But all families have their arguments, quarrells and disagreements, and living together means we're often fed up with one another. It's easy to forget all they've done for us and most of us take our family for granted, not showing our thanks and appreciation.

'Dedicated To The Ones I Love' is an anthology of poetry for the family. The poems inside are all about love for the family - the love we often forget to show. The poets have written down these feelings, letting their family know just how much they really mean.

# CONTENTS

# THE POEMS

# ENTWINED

The times we laughed and the times we cried
are all mapped out in my head.
You were my guide, my teacher, my friend,
my tears you'd catch, my battles you'd defend.
You incused your name on my susceptible brain
so you'll always be a part of my mind.

You sought out my fears and relieved my pains
used your magic to strengthen my soul.
And now I still see you, when my eyes are shut tight,
did you enter my head one night?
Embroider your image on the back of my lids
to be there forever in my visionless sight?

I bathed in your spirit, inhaled your fire.
You gave me a passion and filled me with life.
Although you're not here I know your presence is near,
and as long as you're entwined around my beating heart
I know we'll never be apart
and never will you leave me.

*Rachel Kendall*

# A TRIBUTE TO MOTHERS EVERYWHERE

Mothers are born to love and devotion,
A sacred promise, remains unbroken,
Thoughtful and gentle and often sentimental,
Saintly in their teaching, yet firm without preaching,
Fighters for justice and the truth,
In this land of freedom, since birth,
A time for laughter, a time for tears,
Patience and tolerance through the years,
Submitting with quiet dignity,
They live in all humility.
No sacrifice is ever too great,
Even in pain, they do not hate,
But forge the human chain of love,
Made strong, by mothers up above.

*Margaret Millyard*

# BLACK WIDOW

Suffocated in so small a life
Stifled by the confines of an emptiness that grows
Her sons have made their way into the world
And desire for motivation slowly goes
When swollen knuckles wash the food
To be consumed by only one
And wrinkled skin with make-up on
Is all the sun can shine upon
The misty scenes through watered eyes
Or photos of a way decayed
Are all that's left of broken dreams
Which in her mind are still replayed
Deep in her heart she surely feels
The separation death reveals
And knows that she must share the blame
For all that sent the man insane
Until at length he went his way
And tenderness discovered
Came too late to save the day.

*Andrew Hodson*

# LISTEN

Life moves so slowly
Time moves so fast
Marriage is so brittle
It wasn't meant to last
My heart beats steadily
My pulse goes so quick
You have sex in the evening
In the morning you are sick
It means something to hold you
It means something to cry in the night
My child gives my life meaning
Your love doesn't make things right

I held out my arms in loneliness
I cried out in fear
As the merry-go-round went past me
I wanted to hold you so near
You say the words 'I love you'
I imagine they are true
But sentences come so easily
And speeches are untrue
Do you listen to what I'm saying
Do you hear the pleas I make
Do you hear my tears within the night
Please listen for pity's sake

I love the man I met
He promised me the moon
It all fell by the wayside
He can't come back too soon
If it's going to finish
Let's end it right now
If we can pick up the pieces
Just please God tell me how?

*Debra Kay-Spencer*

# A NEW FAMILY MEMBER

As I have to give birth in this unnatural way
To our baby son or daughter today
Thinking I would rather feel the pain
And give birth to our (my) baby in the natural way.

But all I could think of in that moment in time
Is our (my) baby going to be born alive?
Even though it's been a difficult experience (and time)
At least when it's born, I know the baby's is mine (ours)

All I can do is wait and see, what the baby's going to be
Then I hear the magic sound all mothers want to hear
The crying sound of your new-born baby which makes you
shed a tear in the corner of your eye.

When finally the anxious and precious moment comes
And you hear the moment when the nurse says it's a girl (boy)
Also it's healthy too, and your loving partner and son
is waiting for you.

I give a little prayer to myself and say Thank You Lord
For this miracle you have given to (me) us
Oh I can't wait for the rest of my family to see
This precious life (girl, boy) the Lord has given to (me) us.
To my husband (partner, father) and my son (brother, sister)
Whom I love just as much for evermore, as one big (new)
happy family.

*Mark Bernard Thorpe*

## BEST FRIENDS

A friend I have who cares a lot.
Has time for me, no matter what,
So if the sky is dull and grey
We meet and sweep the gloom away.

A trouble shared is less by half
'Tis better still to share a laugh!
Always together through thick and thin
One to turn to, when tears begin

Bright years of youth - then years of age
Our parts we play across life's stage,
A friend will share the cup that cheers,
Helping to banish doubt and fears.

When I must tread a weary mile
That friend will be there with a smile,
Such a friend - more precious than gold
From early days, till we grow old

*Gladys Thompson*

# MY TRUE FRIEND

You look at me and even though
I speak no word, you seem to know
Whenever things are on my mind;
You see while others' eyes are blind,
And even when we are apart
I know that I am in your heart,
Your spirit travels to take hold,
And keeps me warm when nights are cold;
Since we were small it's always you
Who somehow always gets me through,
When shadows fall you light the way
And see me through another day;
There is a love that binds our souls
It is this love that makes us whole,
What would I be if not for you?
I would not know just what to do
If suddenly there ceased to be
The one that means so much to me.

*Keri Portingale*

# LOVE'S LESSON

Two lonely people
Ready for love
Young and free
One was me -
Then every night in a bar
Having fun
Every day lounging
In the sun -
Completely under her spell
Heaven at last
        After hell;
Without knowing
Where we were going
So long as together
Tomorrow and forever
I didn't care
So long as she was there;
Only now
I am finding
Love is blinding
It is deceiving
A dream
A scheme
To break your heart,
Right from the start
I should have known
Better to stay alone,
But, I didn't die,
And I rarely cry
        Anymore
Though I still adore her
Love keeps me
        Waiting for her.

*Thomas C Ryemarsh*

# TOMORROW'S CHILD

Whilst Governments fall and new ones come,
My youngest grandchild sucks her thumb,
But not for comfort,
No not she!
Who sits in contemplation
Of our future world to be;
All knowledge is hers at the tender age of three:
Blue eyes so wise
Look straight through me
To the dawn of this new Aquarian Age
That awaits her performance centre stage.

Though wars still declare the reign of the 'Beast',
And time-bombs tick in the Middle East,
The new generation
Child of today,
Comes with love to fashion
Anew our world of clay
As old thought-patterns are crushed and cast away.
Though today, she may
Still seem to some
But a tiny child who sucks her thumb,
Tomorrow, she'll lead us through the Millennium.

*C Warren-Gash*

# MY BEST FRIEND

She's just a little chihuahua,
Only standing twelve inches high.
They say that a dog is 'man's best friend'
And I know the reason why.

She's a very proud little beauty,
Trained to the highest degree.
Her rosette claimed her third in her class
From that posh place starting with 'C'.

She chases the cats from the garden
When they lie in the shade of the trees.
Then out comes the brush and powder
'Cause they always leave her their fleas.

I wouldn't say she was faddy.
Just a very selective strain.
She only eats what she fancies
And never goes out in the rain.

She knows it's time for bye-byes
When I go round locking the doors.
I know I have to share my room
With a dear little dog that snores.

She gives me love and devotion
And I give her loving care.
Greeting me home from a weary day
My best little friend is there.

*Marie Wood*

# BIRTH

My son. I have seen wonder through your eyes,
My rebirth through your birth.
Conceived in love,
Received with love,
You, the perfect gift of love.

Now in your adulthood
You too will be enriched,
Your child, your re-creation.
You will feel the pangs of love
Reaching to infinity.
You will do anything
For this precious being,
So beautiful, so intricate
You cannot believe he is.
This tiny baby, your fruition,
Perfection, complete.
Your new view of the familiar world.
Your rebirth and realisation of purpose.

*Joan Marlow*

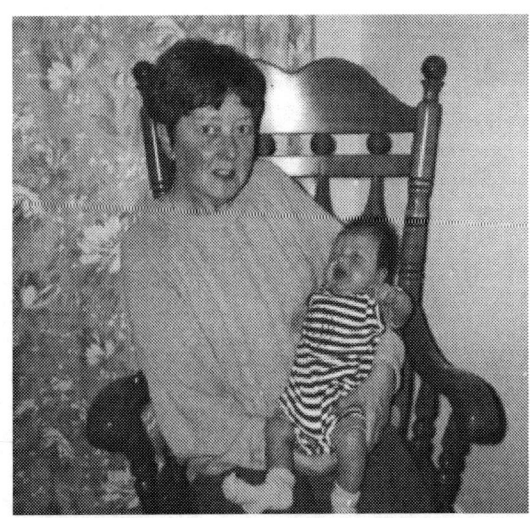

## LOVE'S ETERNAL QUEST

In you I've found a love devine
Ageless and unbound by time
Beyond the grave love will endure
This I know . . . I think . . . I'm sure
That after death our souls will meet
And we'll be together on a seat
From this cosy perch on high
We'll watch the other souls go by
Then we will chose another life
With less trouble, with less strife
Down we will come from above
Eternal in our search for love
Regained flesh . . . rekindled desire
Hearts aflame . . . souls afire
This love for you, inside of me
Will last through all eternity

*April Thorne*

# MY MOTHER

Though my mother has long been gone
Her memory still lingers on
When I cried she would comfort me
By cuddling me upon her knee
Her smile was warm and tender to
And she made me glad in stead of blue

She made me pretty clothes to wear
put pretty ribbons in my hair
She would show me off to all her friends
I thought those days would never end
She was kind and gentle and loved by all
when I was with her I felt ten feet tall

Now she has gone I am sad to say
But in my heart she will always stay
I would give all to have her back again
Because she was a living gem
I have photos of mum to keep and treasure
And I think of her with lots of pleasure

*Rita Hough*

## PUT YOUR ARMS ABOUT ME

Sky is dark and stormy
Like the recesses of my mind
How could you be so cruel?
How could you be so unkind?
I see you through a veil of tears
Why are you mean to me
What have I done, I want to know
Have you no love for me?

Please put your arms about me
Let's make another start
Just tell me that you love me
Hold me to your heart
Hard to know where we went wrong
Too busy or too tired
Can't forget we ever loved
If I said that . . . I lied

Is there a misunderstanding?
Seems I get the blame
I can tell you here and now
Love is not a game
There's never been another
From moment that we met
Surely there's a reason
Your heart's against me set

*Dorothy Joan Sheehan*

# MY DAUGHTER AND HER LOVE

If I were the richest woman,
With all the worldly treasures.
If the heaven and stars were mine,
With the rainbow for my leisure.
If I could hold the sunbeams,
And carry the moon at night,
To warm my life forever,
And keep my darkness bright.
I would not have *all* the treasures
These I already have.
For the priceless gift ever given to me,
Is, 'my daughter and her love'.

*Helen Laurel*

# FRIEND

A friend in need is a friend indeed
as the saying goes, a friend you do need
Friends we can choose
but families we cannot lose

One can use a friend's shoulder
to cry on and be bolder
Families tend to be very emotional
and are never reasonable or rational

They always want to judge you
while a friend simply loves you
You become a good companion
without a tied down union

To a friend you can always say sorry
to a family the word 'sorry' is a worry
To a friend you can always say no
to a family it cannot be so

A friend could be your lover too
but your spouse may not be a friend too
Families you have always to woo
a friend doesn't mind you saying boo

With families you worry about feelings
with a friend you can have easy dealings
A friend may laugh at your silly joke
but the family may think you are a jerk

Families can make life difficult
with a friend you can consult
So to a friend I will go always
loving my family too always

*Albert Moses*

30

## OUR BEST FRIEND

Everyone says they love him.
He's a good friend to us all.
So why do we pretend we're out
When he attempts to call?

It isn't as if we hate him.
He hasn't got BO
It's just when he comes round to tea
It's hard to make him go.

He doesn't smoke or swear or drink.
He doesn't kick the cat.
In fact he's really well behaved.
We all agree on that.

But when he's drunk his fifteenth cup
And eaten all your cake
And watched five of your videos
He's pretty hard to take.

But we do like him to visit.
He's a poppet. He's a dear.
And he's welcome any time next week
So sad we won't be here.

But I'm sure the Browns will love him
And treat him as their own
And meanwhile we are off to Spain
To find another home.

*Jo Gray*

# YOU DID MORE

You did more
than offer friendship
You did more
than show you care
Held out loving arms to hold me
Ran your fingers through my hair.

You did more
than I had asked for
You did more
than I had known
Wrote of deep love to your dearest
That I wasn't on my own.

You did more
than any other
You did more
and others knew
Saw the way we were together
A fairy tale to misconstrue?

You did more
than I could cope with
You did more
than 'just a friend'
Kept me thinking, did you love me?
But no, there's nothing, here's the end.

*Sarah Threadkell*

# MOTHER

Mother sits in her rocking chair
Forwards and backwards she rocks all day
Never complains happy alone
Her own little kingdom
Her own little throne
Always a smile and a cheery hello
As her knitting needles move to and fro
A hard life has passed her by
She'll reminisce and give a sigh
Wealth's no good to me
My days have gone by
You can't take it with you when you die
A heart of gold you really had
Always there through good and bad
This sad day your life is to cease
Waiting to pass to a land of peace
You raise a smile and whisper thanks
Forever grateful you held our hands
As your eyes close we give praise
For the years and the memories we'll never erase

*Joyce Lawson*

## COCKTAIL PARTY

If I should ever come to myself again
       And experience agony,
Could transmit across gulfs
       With my eyes,
Reach outstretched suppliant hands
       To the further shores of yourself,
Would you receive?

If I spoke so loud I said nothing
       Would you begin to believe
I had something to say
       Such as *take me away from this place*
or *can't we go home*
       or *who are these people*
or *let us get married again?*

Sometimes I shout *who are you*
       or *when did we die*
and *come back*
       But no-one is listening then -
Not even myself. I am deaf
       Of too much shouting and words
That cannot even make me turn my head.

*Alasdair Aston*

# SMILE AND THE WHOLE WORLD SMILES WITH YOU

One day I saw a lonely face
whilst walking down the street,
A face so full of sorrow,
a face so hard to greet.
And in this lonely face I saw,
such pain and anguish show,
The hardship of a life so sad
that you and I won't know.
For whilst we have each other,
the loneliness is bare,
So I smiled into the lonely face
as if to say 'I care'.
And then I saw a glimmer
of hope shine through those eyes
And briefly, oh, so briefly,
I thought I saw a smile.
And now I walk back down the street,
a smile for all to see
And I look at all the lonely faces
smiling back at me.

*Angela Jane Norris*

# THE STAR OF MY WORLD

You came to me one crisp January day
Through all the pain and tears
You lay there gurgling and crying
A miracle in my arms

You are my star, my world, my all
With your light brown hair and eyes
Your rosy cheeks and silly chatter
You have filled a gaping chasm
And given me a love of life

Sophie my beautiful one
How deep is love, I can never explain
If fills the universe,
All the planets, stars and moons

God bless all the children
You are our past, present and future
One day you will leave us
To find your own paths in life
But for now, Sophie, stay with me
Forever our hearts are entwined

I love you darling
You are the star of my world

*Cate Arculeo*

# GRANDSON

Silently I peer over the brim
Of satin fringed moses basket
To spy a treasure lying there
Your daddy's long body
Crowned in mummy's raven hair
Well fed and watered
Growing so strong
Safely cocooned in a family bond
Innocent eyes sparkle with fun
Evoke sweet memories of our own
Little one
Now to go sleep my handsome boy
You will always be a source of
Pride and joy.

*R D Allin*

# WHEN GOOD FRIENDS CHANGE

When I was younger, and I had a very good friend,
Someone I thought I could trust in, and depend.

We shared and we cared, whilst we did a lot of things together,
There were plenty of laughs, whatever the weather.

She vowed, that whatever the changes would be,
She would always go on being, a good friend to me.

We are both older now, and so much wiser in life,
We've both had our troubles, and gone through some strife.

Now troubles affect people, in different ways,
Sadly we no longer see each other, these days.

We've both moved on, and have families of our own,
And although I would like to see her, she prefers to be left alone.

I wish her well, and I feel it is such a shame,
That two friends as close as we were, are no longer the same.

But I can keep the happy memories, of how things used to be,
Because we have to go forward, I'm sure anyone would agree.

We march into the future, but no-one ever knows,
What lies ahead on our path, or what will blossom or what will grow.

So whatever new friends I make now, I am wary and this is true,
Because I know that good friends can change, and the only
                    friend that you can depend on is you.

*Christine Bolton-Pearson*

## MY WORLD

My love I stand here watching you now
My life will be brighter today somehow
My world will never be quite the same
My love is sincere and never a game
My life is for you and for us to share
My world is open and will always be there
My love I offer you my world in my life
My life is your love shared as man and wife
My wife is my love, my world, my life.

*James E Royle*

# MARTIN - MY DEAR FRIEND

*(Dedicated to my best friend Martin Pont who died
in tragic circumstances on February 4th 1970 aged 16)*

Today I look down and remember a friend,
A friend I shall never forget,
And now he has left us -
Gone forever -
Whilst the grave for him is set.

So loved by all of us,
So missed by all,
Yet my tears won't bring him back.
Never again will we meet again.
My life is oh so sad.

Why did this world take my friend?
My friend above all others,
Why was it his life which had to end
In such sudden departure.

Weeping over him,
God, how I miss him,
Martin - my dear friend.

*Mark Newson*

# LEFT ALONE

The room is dark and I am cold
Not by the weather, but the lonely feeling inside
Just a few short weeks ago I was surrounded
By colleagues, acquaintances and friends
But my world has dramatically changed
And I am left wondering, pondering contemplating
How were the ties of friendship severed?
Now left as a forgotten person, an empty chair
The passing of time swiftly and decisively
Removing me to unmemorable history
Like some uneventful landmark left to decay and rot
I need to be rebuilt, mentally, loved and encouraged

Where are those friends who were there for the good times
No call, no visit, no letter and no bonding
Unlike a marriage friends need have no commitment
In sickness and in health, for the good times and now the bad
Am I sinking into despair, paranoid about my predicament?
For it is no longer unusual to be redundant
But how I feel the stigma has washed over my friends
Like an infectious plague keeping me isolated
Should I make the first move, stand proud and ring
Head held high, positive, cheerful, even light-hearted!
But to what end, for what response, what gain
I am so unsure what friends are, or indeed what I want them to be!

*Philip M Smith*

# FRIENDSHIP
*(Dedicated to Pam Wilson)*

We have many happy memories
yet days of endless pain
weeks of sunshine and laughter
nights of darkness and rain,
there are dreams we want to hold on to
and things we would rather forget
secrets we've shared with each other
problems with which we have met.
There are mistakes of which we've made many
enemies! Perhaps just a few
but let's put all that behind us
as there's a future we've yet to view
so let's pray for that sunshine
and laughter
wave goodbye to the sorrow and pain
because there's one thing I know for certain
my best friend you will always remain.

*Pauline Fogerty*

# FRIENDSHIP

Retrospective memories strike uninvited
They enter and exit my existence.
Linear journeys intersected by other's consciousness
Each one contributes and takes away.
Some are sybaritic
Pleasureable trace decays remain.
Recalled at unexpected moments
Triggers of time.
Perfume, the scent of soap, the elderberry's pungence
Evoke peaks and troughs of emotion.
Dappled memories of faces and places
Filter reality's richness.
Visitations occur in dreams
Deceased grandparents, faces from childhood.
Faces I have yet to meet
Who can tell?
Some have shared tears, mostly laughter's echo remains
To enrich experience and exorcise emotion.
Problems shared, united by acquaintance
Bestowal of the ultimate gift
Friendship.

*Lynda Thwaites*

# MOTHER, I FORGOT TO TELL YOU

Hankering for the cushion chair by the
fire: beams of orange light flickering through
the half-net curtain of the tiny window.

A most treasured diploma in glass frame
on wall. Other trinkets and ornaments of
endearment. The statuettes of matching dogs so
lovingly placed each side of the fireplace.

Many childhoods were shared here.
I remember the repetitive swish of the brush.
The continual adjusting of the mat below the
stairs. The thick bulging wires leading right
to the wireless and left to the television set.

The screech of our mother's voice -
'What are you doing up there? Come down!'
The defiance - as she chased me up the road to
the cheers and shouts of the men in the poultry
factory over.

Mother, I forgot to tell you . . .

    . . . I was in a grand house. Everything
    immaculate and expensive. Dinner served on
    a long table with crispy white table cloth.
    The conservation so stilted and correct.
    I longed to . . . transport across the expanse
    of water and be there in that cushion chair.

And when I sat again after a hearty welcome. Young ones
round my feet to know their gifts. I wanted to say about
that warmth and love I didn't find elsewhere. But the
words got lost in the urgency of time. 'Go up and see
your dad. I'll send out for a cake. Come on and we'll
have a cuppa.'

Mother, I forgot to tell you . . . your house had it all.

*Marie McCarthy*

## FAMILIES

Families! What a nightmare,
A millstone like no other.
Especially, as in my case,
If you're the little baby brother.

Never, ever to be consulted,
Told what to do and where to be.
Don't you realise non-consultation
Insults my mentality.

Unsubtle innuendo,
Inherited from your Father.
It's not my fault you peaked so early on
And never progressed any farther.

Look! I'll fight for socialism if I want,
My independence makes me proud.
I'm no longer wearing nappies,
I'm forty-seven years old for crying out loud!

*Bruce Ward*

## OUR PLAY

Life is really one big act,
Not revealing our true role,
Putting on a face, in fact
Hiding what's in our soul.

'How are you' families say?
To which we answer 'I'm fine,'
Even though it's a bad day,
And we're sad with hearts that pine.

In truth do we ever say
I'm sad, and ill, and lonely,
Being honest may not pay,
Family say if only

You would try and let us care
For you, with wisdom, and love,
Families have time to spare,
With aid of spirits above.

Be yourself, discard the mask,
Your natural self please be,
You then help us with our task,
Open your heart and you'll see

Life is full of love and joy,
See the dear ones all around,
Like a child with a new toy,
With new vigour you'll abound.

*Suzane Joy Golding*

## ABSENT HUSBAND

I gave you the best years, of my life.
They were filled with worry, sweat, tears, strife.
Really - was I such an awful ugly wife.

I darned your socks, washed your clothes.
Bathed your troubles, heard your woes.
Nursed the babies, tendered their needs.
Watched them grow. Young love go.

Christmases came. Christmases went.
The increased pressure left spirits bent.
Worked so hard to keep you pleased,
four jobs together, knocked me down on my knees.

The house must be spotless, no toys to be seen.
You always walked out impeccably clean.
Pockets filled with money to burn.
Took me years, the lesson to learn.

You never looked back, to see me left there.
Years of unhappiness, you just didn't care.
I cared for the home, our children,
my husband. Never there.

Gone down the pub. Your god was the beer,
buying rounds. Full of good cheer *'Friends'* around you.
Did you feel good, did you feel great?
The feeling you got down the pub, I would hate.

It's false, it's empty. Never could last,
how much does it cost? That big empty glass.
Measures one pint, any men think!
Bottomless pit; as they pour down the drink.

The true cost, the ones they forgot
birthdays, sorrows, kindness, pain,
smiles devotion, in fact all the lot.
Quick check in the mirror.
Down the pub absent husband, will trot.

*E B Whitmore*

## FRIENDSHIP AND LOVE

To have the loyalty of friends,
And the love of a family,
One must be willing, to give both in return,
Without any reservations.

To give help when it's needed,
Love when it's wanted,
For helping and loving others,
Brings its own reward.

If you have friends, you have everything,
With family love you have the world,
Without either, you would have nothing,
Life would be meaningless.

*Maud Eleanor Hobbs*

# BEYOND THE GRAVE

What happens to us when we die
And leave this earth we know so well?
Do we straight to heaven go
Or straight down into hell?
No my friends, it's not so simple
To die is such an easy thing,
The way we die is chosen for us
By He who governs everything.
You cannot say, 'I will not go,'
Because you're not at peace,
It makes no difference who you are,
He calls, your heart will surely cease.
When He calls you from this life
The body fails, and dies,
Your soul detaches from the shell
And straight to heaven flies.
The shell is then burned, as a cinder,
Or buried in the ground,
All mortal use for it has gone,
Your soul, a better home has found.
You travel far above this earth
To a place of rest and peace
Where pain and sorrow are not known
And there you bide till troubles cease,
For, if in trying not to go
You leave this life in sorrow,
In God's pastures up on high
You cannot walk tomorrow.
So be content with what you have
Let not your passing fear you,
For when we pass along the way
His hand is surely near you.

*R L Shipp*

# ODE TO MY MOTHER

In my earliest memory you are there
Someone to love me, someone to care,
Green eyes shining from a smiling face
When I was in trouble you'd plead my case,
Julia Madison my wonderful mother
Always there for me and my brother,
Since you became my father's wife
You've had some disasters in your life,
A car crash left you with a broken neck
Was your life over, were you a wreck,
No you weren't beaten you put up a fight
One step at a time first left then right,
A few years later you had an electric shock
Hand held in the water, your body rigid like rock,
Did you worry about your life passing by
No your thoughts were for me, not if you would die,
As the years pass our bond's become stronger
And I know that one day you won't be there no longer,
I hope that time is far away
And by my side you will always stay,
My love for you couldn't be greater
My mum, my mother, my mama, my mater.

*Dawn 'Madison' Kerr*

# OLD PALS, YOUNG MINDS

Hugging corners, sporting ties,
friendly banter, friendly lies,
swatting summer's wrestless flies,
great pals,
Reminisce, our schoolboy days,
young and wild, wayward strays,
striding youths, crazy ways
timing waits.

Life played his trump, he only can,
the boy runs off, to meet the man,
a familiar pose, a frequent plan,
enter life,
A hand of rain, a drop of tears,
a christened babe, tingling fears,
a shoulder look, a bunch of years,
what change.

Seaside lollies, melting fast,
offspring laughing, stretching past,
September breeze, ushers past,
slight warning,
Old pals cluster, at my arm,
young again, but much too calm,
parting slaps, now show a palm,
yesteryears, tyrant boys:

*I MacLaren*

# THE ROSE

Do you remember the rose you gave me
      One summer's day?
You promised that you'd always love me
      Come what may.
But summer sunshine faded fast
And when the chill autumnal blast
Surrounded us in mist at last,
      You went away.

We walked among the summer roses
      Hand in hand;
What caused our love to change I'll never
      Understand.
You handed me the crimson flower
That you had broken from the bower
In that sweet, oft' remembered hour
      In fairyland.

The rose was fresh and fragrant with
      The morning dew;
I kept it pressed close to my heart
      For love of you.
Your love has faded long ago,
And in the cold December snow,
The rose that I had cherished so
      Has faded too.

*Charles McSherry*

## OLD PALS

I was eighteen when I first met Olive,
A real Canadian Gal.
We became the very best of friends
And called each other pal.
With her parents she came to England,
About nineteen thirty four,
And we worked together for several years,
Until parted by the war.
She joined the Canadian Air Force,
Quite early in World War Two,
Then later returned to Canada
To the country that she knew.
Olive married and had five children,
Three were girls and two were boys.
She wrote to me with all her news,
Her sorrows and her joys.
She told me all about Canada,
The homeland she held so dear,
And described the Calgary Stampede,
That is held there every year.
In the eighties she stopped writing,
No more letters came for me,
Although I still tried to keep in touch,
Until nineteen ninety three.
I wonder where she is now,
That real Canadian Gal,
Who was once my very dearest friend,
And called me her old pal.

*Ivy Neville*

## IN THE MIDST OF MIND

In the midst of mind a memory's stirring,
Of what could have been keeps recurring,
But if we could change life's fated path
Would we enjoy the aftermath.

Daily we tread where others dread,
And in doing so forge on ahead,
There are times when we look back
At what we had then, and now lack

And often wish we had spoke up
When others stole a sip from our cup,
Then when we realise the cup is drained
Our friendships are severely strained.

*Jack Ellis*

## IMAGINING

Imagining creates a wishful lie
And self deluding dreams in my mind's eye.
Within a dark place, buried deep inside
I do endeavour yearnings there to hide.
My daily life drifts on in simple style
But in my heart I hold a secret smile.
The person I portray is dull and plain
So full of indecision, doubt and pain
Yet when emotions deep are running high
Exposure of the truth I can't deny.
I then accept the being wished by me
Acknowledge all the passion, set it free.
The hidden woman's confident, walks tall,
Ambitious, independent, loved by all,
Desire radiates from every pore
Provocative, alluring, slim, so sure.
Sometimes she unrestricted, has free rein,
Then sense prevails, she's confined once again
Imagining is all that's left to see,
And looking through my inner eye at me.

*Christine Boden*

## LET ME IN

I love you very deeply, do you love me?
Together for always that's how it's meant to be
We live together, eat together, are together every day
But I need more from this life, I need you in a different way
I need you to need me the way that I need you
I need you here beside me in everything I do
You seem to live your own life without needing me there
You keep your feelings hidden and seem unwilling to share
All that you are and everything you want to be
You keep away hidden so that I cannot see
I want to feel all your pain as well as all your joy
I don't want picking up and putting down like some old favourite toy
Show me that you love me, show the world you care
Let me into your life, I love you and really need to share
Please do not shut me out, I cannot stand the pain
No matter who or what you are my feelings can never wane
I need you now and always, please be there for me
Let our love light up this world for everyone to see.

*J Gatenby*

# MY MOTHER'S ANGEL

An angel came from heaven,
She whispered in my ear,
Don't worry about your loving mum,
She's happy over here.

Each day the sun will shine on you,
And you will smile again,
I know your mother loves you,
So wait for her again.

When you're asleep she'll visit you,
And slip into your dreams.
To leave you lovely thoughts of her,
Life isn't what it seems.

Do live your life, and guard it well,
This is your mother's wish,
I've given you her message dear,
Now I leave you with her kiss.

Don't forget these precious words,
They will guide you on your way.
Keep them close beside you,
And think of *Mum* each day.

*Elsie May Hellon*

# WHAT IS LOVE?

What is love? The magic
Of someone close to you.
Hold a baby in your arms,
Soft and warm it's very true.

Children, children precious,
To love and fill your day
With happiness and laughter
All along life's way.

Love for nature in her beauty,
The sky, the sea, the land.
A courting couple sharing love,
Walking hand in hand.

Love of laughter, smiling eyes,
Love for your family,
To kiss and say 'I love you,
You mean so much to me.'

Love can come in many ways,
A dear friend's love to share.
A garden in the summertime,
God's love is everywhere.

Day by day a prayer to say
To the Lord above,
Thank you God for giving us
The joy of sharing love.

*Patricia Catling*

## A FAMILY

A family unit is made of many generations
A little group of two or three or a mixture of many nations,
Brothers and sisters, nephews and nieces,
A large jigsaw puzzle of many pieces.

Often remembered, sometimes at war,
A shoulder to cry on, the odd little flaw,
Family reunions, breakfast in bed,
Funerals and weddings, tears always shed.

A comforting letter when you're miles away from home,
The voice of reassurance when you telephone,
Someone to look up to when you need advice,
Sometimes we have arguments but mostly we are nice.

So let's raise our glasses and make a small toast
And give thanks today to what matters most,
We may not have money but no matter what
Here's to our riches - the family we've got.

*Tracy Benjafield*

# MUM

What have I achieved in life, my old Mum said to me.
And I cast my mind back to the days when I sat upon her knee.
Times were hard in years gone by, when she was in her youth
I don't know how she managed and that surely is the truth.

My Dad, he was a miner, a fine and honest man.
Together they would sit and talk, for the future plan.
Mum cared for all her family, whether kith or kin,
To her they came from far and near, if trouble they were in.

Small of stature, strong of will, forgiving nature for those
                                        who did her ill.
She dealt with life's hardships and kept on trying.
Though it broke her heart, she nursed my Dad, as he was dying.

And what of her now, when she's old and pale, her legs
                            are bandaged and her sight has failed.
She looks into the fire with unseeing eyes, and when she's
                                alone, I'm sure that she cries.
Yet she's quick of wit and smart of mind, no worldly wealth,
                                but she's still as kind.
She loves her children more than ever, and no-one can
                            fool her, she's still as clever.

There may be those in the Hall of Fame who are easily
                                recognised by their name.
Their achievements, all the world can measure, but in my Mum
                                    I have a treasure.

As I see her face at the window pane then she walks toward
                            me slowly, hands on her white cane.
When I watch her mouth form a welcoming smile and know
                        however weary she would walk a mile,
To help me on my way,
Care for me each day.
Warm me when I'm cold
And shelter me though she's old.

I gave her no answer when the question she did ask.
But she has no need to wonder or set herself a task.
Like her I will have conquered the world, at eighty three
If I mean as much to my daughter, as my Mum means to me.

*Annette Walker*

# ARE YOU PROUD OF ME

I sometimes feel that I don't make you happy
You're disappointed with what I've done with my life
But can't you see how well I'm getting by on my own?
Can't you see I'm happy with my life?

I know I can do more and I will when I'm ready
For now I've got a daughter to care for
Can't you see what a good job I'm doing as a mother?
Can't you see I give her everything she needs and more?

I don't know what to do to make you happy
And even if all I do is raise a child on my own
Wouldn't that be good enough for my own parents?
Why is it I sometimes feel so alone?

If I could go back in time and change anything I wouldn't
I know you're not happy with the things I choose to do
But even though I love you both so much
I wouldn't change a thing not even for you

You looked after and cared for me when I was little
You brought me up with values, strength and believing my heart

I am the way I am because of your parental judgement
I've grown to be polite, open-minded and smart

I'm a young woman now, please trust my judgement
This is my life and I'll live it how I want to
I hope you'll understand it's what's best for me
Then one day you might turn and say 'We're proud of you.'

*Carly Gilchrist*

# JUDE

It's a few years now since we said goodbye,
Why should one so young suddenly die,
Full of life - a very special friend,
I miss you.

A colleague at work like a sister you became,
In so many ways we were just the same,
Sharing secrets - someone to talk to,
I miss you.

Fond memories I keep of the times we had,
Most of them happy, some of them sad,
Special moments together - laughter and joy,
I miss you.

An illness it was that took you away,
Oh! How I cried that July day,
It's lonely without you - empty and dark
I miss you.

Never to be forgotten your memory will stay,
I still smell your perfume and think of you each day,
Jude my dear friend so special were you,
I miss you so much - I really do.

*Amanda S Holland*

## OUR FRIENDS

Good friends are rare,
Returning our love with care,
Full of fun and full of life,
A stalwart help in daily strife.
Some friends are timid and quiet,
And would never cause a riot.

Others are rather touchy,
With tempers sometimes crusty,
People are never quite the same,
Different in their living.
And certainly in their *giving*,
A mixed diet is considered healthy,
And so are different friends,
And definitely more entertaining.

*Margaret White*

# FOREVER ALONE

Fear built up steadily,
Once controllable, not even noticeable,
Now undisguisable;
Seeping through despite
the pathetic home-made defences;
The barriers against the pain.
Then the weak smile falters a little too soon,
She starts to cry; then
runs from him without explanation.
His anger is not hidden,
Yet he cares for no-one but himself,
He does not follow her,
She is alone once more.

*Niki Foxwell*

# FORBIDDEN LOVE

The sun is up early these days of July,
I watch from your window the glow in the sky.
It chases the shadows from your windowsill
Then lights up the room where you lie warm and still.

Soon it is drinking the dew from your lawn.
It tells me - 'My darling'

It's time I was gone.

*Peter Hewitt*

# OUR FRIENDSHIP

Our friendship is a strange one;
of joy and magic too,
The time we spend together's fun,
I love to be with you.

Our friendship is built on trust;
and the secrets that we share,
When I have a problem,
it's you who's always there.

Our friendship is precious;
our caring is so deep,
Sharing all we'll ever have;
this bond I hope we'll keep.

*C Long*

# AWAKE

I lie awake, in search of you
Awaiting your caress
But for now I only touch you in my dreams
For the night parts us and becomes my hatred

Thinking of you, awake I lie
Dependant upon your kiss
I can only imagine your love inside
As dawn creeps ever nearer and becomes my all

Dreaming of you, I lie still, silent
Drifting into your eyes
I am only dreaming
But day arrives, and I awake, for I will see you once more

*Amanda Bruce*

# FEELINGS SHARED

An explosion of your feelings,
unsure whether you are being understood,
but still glad to talk.

Such a long search to find understanding
when discovered,
Sends a wave of relief right through you.

The knowledge that there is always
someone there to listen,
Always caring, always understanding, always feeling.

Always there to take you higher in yourself,
Always able to guide your heart,
Always able to raise a smile.

Draining all the stress from your body
makes you feel free from the chains
that have kept you from living.

But all those feelings from the past
come back to haunt you,
punishing your newly discovered happiness.

But that someone is there once more,
with the strength to keep you from falling
to the depth of your inner turmoil.

Picked up and carried by the words
of reality and tenderness,
to a point where you know you are understood.

*C C Dick*

# TWENTY TWO YEARS

For twenty two years we've been married
For twenty two years our burdens you have carried
And all this time your love's never faltered
Along with dedication that didn't ever alter

You raised our children without complain
And gave them all without restraint
For twenty two years you've stayed with me
Showered us with love for all to see

All through this time you never doubted
Never got angry and never shouted
You rained upon us a love so divine
So strong and powerful that it did shine

Whatever we wanted you did provide
Never once did I see you hide
You were always there right at the front
To give us everything we ever did want

And my darling you were always strong
Even when you knew we were wrong
I love you so from the bottom of my heart
Because in my life you have played a large part

What can I say what can I do
There will never be another you
Words fail me so good that you are
I'll love you forever both near and afar

*Harriet Wright*

# FAMILY

The bond that ties us sees us through
When times bring grief and pain
You know there's always someone there
Till you are strong again

The kindly thoughts, the loving smile
All brighten up the day
It's good to know that all the while
They are not far away
In thought and deed, and this I know
That, come what may, it's sure
The love and thoughts of those who care
Make living so much more.

For it keeps the happy times alive
It helps when things go wrong.
So, God Bless you, happy families
May you stay forever strong.

*Doris Cowie*

# REFLECTIONS

As I'm getting older,
  My life moves by, so fast,
I take the time to reflect upon,
  Fond memories of my past.

My babies, born when I was young,
  Their giggles and their cries,
Their first few steps, their open love,
  I hear my Mother's sighs.

My very own wonderful childhood,
  I remember falling over, and how,
My Mum would cuddle the hurt away,
  I wish she could cuddle me now.

My husband always by my side,
  Has been enough to see me through,
The problems of my grown up years,
  Believe me, there's been a few.

Many people have passed through my life,
  I still have friends, made in school,
Technicolour memories they've given to me,
  and with love, I remember them all.

*Brenda Barker*

## MEMORIES ARE TREASURED THOUGHTS

Memories are lovely thoughts, that linger in your mind
A little store of treasures, of places, and people that were kind.

It's funny how we 'turn the key', and remember those happy days
Each little thought is brought to life, in so many different ways.

It may be something that we see, or things that people say
Then all at once we remember, things we did, one day.

So don't be sad and lonely, when you've had a trying day
Just unlock those 'lovely memories', that you have stored away.

*Victor R Travis*

# THE TORCH OF LOVE

For the child who skipped along the path
On that faded and old photograph
Life still remains vibrantly strong
Interesting to live enjoy and belong.

As a Grandma now, looking back again
Not much to change, but so much to retain.
Loving support from a really good man
When life did not always run to plan.

Pleasures from family's growing years.
Hopes and doubts, and childhood fears;
Joy of weddings and then the sorrow
The house will be much emptier tomorrow.

With so much shared within the home,
Those bonds remain as siblings roam.
Love and understandings still bind,
And in those darkest hours remind.

For roles may change and names as well
Yet within each heart memories dwell.
Passing love on to a new generation
Nurturing respect for each situation.

As living in this more expectant age
Frustration can give way to rage.
Violent intolerance, negative unrest,
Old ways lost, or at best just guessed.

Strong family values can again restore,
Bring peace and hope to life once more
Forgiveness, trust, love and respect,
Greater communication, less neglect.

So learning, we achieve our plans
As experience guides with loving hands.
That torch of love rekindles the flame
And hindsight becomes more than a name.

*H D Hensman*

# SHOP WINDOWS

There is that ghostly reflection
Familiar in a striking way.
Stooping in aged recollection
As if she has something to say.
Hovers, then steps on the pavement
Shop window mirrors her stride,
Shrugs, now making a statement
The mac' hangs down without pride.
Where has that sprightly young woman
Gone with her swaggering style,
When a toss of the head could summon
And a twinkling eye would beguile.
Why did she plan for tomorrow
And miss what she had in the day.
Who will be left to follow,
Then the rain washed the shadow away.

*Trish Birtill*

## MUM

Memories held in hands of time
Now trapped within the past
A part of me no longer mine
Why do you fade so fast

Moments shared now stand alone
And slowly drift away
Although my past may turn to stone
I'll cherish every day.

With thoughts of you close by my side
I will not break in two
For in my heart I know I'll find
The memory that was you.

*Lindsey Newrick*

# UNTITLED

When I love you
Will you still be my friend
when I need you
can I count on you
Or is this the end

If when I disappoint you
Will you forgive me
or am I to wander
A cast out adrift on the sea

Are the tears of my eyes
For you or for me
I never meant to hurt you
But somehow you've set me free
My love and my faith for you
Are more than twinkling stars above

I am still in love with you
Are you surprised
That love is forever
A lasting pure river
When I love you
Will you still be my friend

*Denis Manley*

## ODE TO EMMA

Little girls are special
a treasure to adore
just give her lots of love and hugs
she'll give you so much more.

She'll bring you joy with each day
you'll worry all the while
but you can't deny she's adorable
just look at how she smiles.

This is Emma Wilson
and I'm sure you'll all agree
she certainly is a treasure
a joy for all to see.

*Dorothy Johnstone*

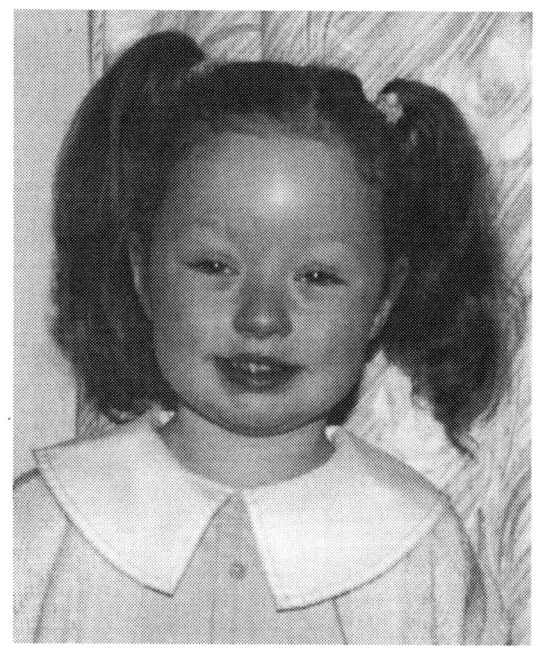

# FRIENDSHIP'S KISS - FRIENDSHIP'S WISH

I was down
depressed and lonely
you showed me affection
I took it
held it to my lips
and caressed it
revelling in its caring touch
not thinking whence it came
it did not matter
I was needed
wanted
love was mine
but for a moment
I should not have lingered
with the mirage
it left me empty
soulless
more alone than before.

*Paula Edwards*

# THE DAFFODILS

Winter blues set in this year
a month too soon for this poor soul.
February *was* the month to fear
and go to ground, just like a mole.
Conscious that I'm growing old
I now succumb to merest cold.

The New Year's only just begun,
with freezing winds and ice and snow.
Oh, how I long for scorching sun
to make my face and body glow,
but all I see are skies of grey
from morn till eve of each long day.

My spirits sink when I'm alone
content no more with self comp'ny.
Placidity has now up and flown
leaving an introspective me
wondering what is held in store.
Will happiness return once more?

While wallowing in this state of gloom
came a ring upon the front door bell.
Then an angel sweet lit up the room -
whose presence always weaves a spell -
with gentle kiss and warming hug.
Her tender eyes my heartstrings tug.

And in her hand she held some flowers
of brightest gold, like rays of sun,
to cheer me through the dreary hours;
a lovely keepsake when she's gone.
For me a token, every day,
of her love while she's away.

*Horace Gamble*

# FRIENDS AND FAMILIES

'Class' divides people who could have been great friends,
It's an unsightly shadow that hovers over generations,
Who or what will get hurt next as it descends,
On a simple kind person with no expectations.

Some families consider themselves better than the next,
Each thought produces a narrow lifestyle,
Of isolation that grows out of context,
And their hearts harden all the while.

Take time my friend to be understanding,
And open your arms in friendship where it has elapsed,
Have no expectations which may seem demanding,
Be relaxed, yourself and allow God to bridge the gaps.

Other families are quite the opposite,
Where love and security binds them together,
And support and concern is a treasured deposit,
In each member's heart that lives on forever.

Kind and encouraging words they often share,
Quality and equality time often spent,
Knowing you're surrounded by people who care,
Loving and kind parents are heaven-sent.

*Dawn Madigan*

# THE ROCK

*(Written for all the friends and family in my life. Especially so, for the eternal memory of Frances and Charles Humphrey)*

The rock is there to guide me, a beacon through the haze
The rock is cooling water when my temper is ablaze.

The rock it is an anchor that keeps me close to shore
On rough and choppy seas it calms me down once more

The rock is my positive energy if I am doubtful for a while
And when I feel lonely the rock it makes me smile.

The rock it is my faith it keeps me going strong
The rock that is a law to keep me safe from wrong

Dear rock I'd like to thank you for being in my heart
And if miles come between us we will never be apart.

*Karena J Key*

# THE AWAKENING

Suddenly, a baby cries in my vigilant ear
yet I, in cosiness, pretend I cannot hear!
Saying to myself, 'It's not my turn yet'!
Not thinking that she is bound to forget,
or, like me, pretends to be asleep still,
knowing that soon I will have had my fill!
Leaving me to rise in bad temper, growling,
to confront the child in the cot cowering!
But at sight of this bundle, eyes so wide,
I feel sorrow and shame deep inside.
I gently lift up and admire this part of me
then all of a sudden in the night I can see
a love from my heart that is rarely shown
and a pride in myself I have never known!
The clearing of a throat from the nearby bed
causes natural curiosity to turn my head.
I see a face in a hand leaning on an elbow,
with two moist eyes in a look I well know!
She pats the sheet where she wants me to lie
we snuggle up, all three, lest a baby cry!

*K F Adamson*

## FOREVER FRIENDS

When you're feeling all sad and alone,
Never fear because I'll be there.
I know it sounds soppy and sad
But there's no other way to describe
The way you feel when you have
A friend, so true and loyal like you.

I know things get hard
Leaving you feeling distressed and confused
Never knowing which is the right way to turn
Beginning to feel like
There's no way out for you
Whenever you're feeling that way
I hope you can feel
That you can turn my way.

I'll be there through it all
No matter what
We'll see it through
Because I'm lucky to have
A friend, so true and loyal like you.

*Naz Latif*

## CONGRATULATIONS

I haven't really told you so for such a long time
but let me say I'm proud of you, and more so
'cos you're mine.
Your sheer determination gets you the very best,
brains and intuition make up for the rest.
Your spirit and your kindness are assets you should cherish,
don't let anyone put you down, for you there's only merit.
So well done Cassie, keep it up
and the future holds no limits,
but most of all enjoy life and don't regret a minute.

Loving you always.

*Brenda Schubert*

# MY PRAYER

Jesus teach me how to pray
I ask of you each day
Jesus teach me how to pray
I don't know what to say

My eyes are closed, I'm on my knees
But not a word I've said
Dear Jesus make me speak my pleas
As I kneel with bowed down head

Dear Jesus, the words are out
Forgive me Lord I pray
My mind is drifting once again
I don't know what to say

I can only say 'Forgive me Lord'
Perhaps that will be enough
I find it all so very hard
To say it off the cuff

Perhaps God will forgive me
If I leave it up to Him,
And keep a minute's silence
Before we finish with a Hymn.

*Vera Hansson*

# A LOYAL COMPANION

Where would we be without our dear friends
In times of trouble when the road knows no end
Someone who will call with a cheery word
And relate to a tale they've not long heard

We've helped each other over the years
Consoled one another when in tears
Much water has run under the bridge since then
I recall as children we'd play in our 'den'

We can choose our friends that is true
A loyal companion I have found in you
We've aged together over the years,
There for each other through our tears, and fears.

Friends are such special people in our lives
Without them life would be hard to survive.
I thank you for the friendship I found in you
Since when we first met, and our friendship grew.

*L Culshaw*

# MUM

You feed me when I'm hungry
give cuddles when I'm tired
bath me when I'm covered in food
your love is so inspired
change my bum when it is dirty
never mind the mess
more washing, drying, ironing
you love me nonetheless
at six months old
I'm too young to say
but in my heart and in my eyes
it's as plain as day
that I love you dearly
for everyone to see
there is no other place
I would rather be

*Chris Bailey*

# PINKY

Leaving hospital, I arrived home.
Tired, I rested, holding my cup of tea.
I looked up, the rear door opened slowly.
In walked a white kitten, tiny, looking so helpless.
It looked at me, pink eyed, climbed on my lap.
Then to my shoulder. He had come to stay.
My best loved pet, my Pinky.
Always there when I arrived home from work.
Sleeping on my feet at night time.
When I worked in the garden,
his gentle jump on my back, to my shoulder,
to rub his head against my ear.
His love. His faithfulness,
his trust when given sherry in warm milk for his flu.
My struggle to knit a jumper
which he clawed to himself and sat upon,
it was his.
Thirteen and a half years we were pals.
Always together, till a liver disease claimed him.
He sat on the shed roof in the morning sunshine.
Every branch of the apple tree next to him held birds,
Birds singing, singing in the most wonderful way,
One of nature's wonders.
Sadly that week Pinky passed on.
My gentle loving pet had gone.

*Evelyn Ida Henfield*

## FOR BEA

I'm funny that way
I keep Christmas cards
from old friends
But
reading the obituary
I realise
there will be an empty space
on my mantelpiece
this Christmas.

Apart from my memories
three snowmen singing carols
are all I have left of you.

*Susan Quinn*

# FURROW

I stare into my mother's face,
To see myself,
And all that is and all that was,
A timeless aid
To see tomorrow's dawn;
How blind I have been.
A glimmer of reflection
In the old woman's eyes,
Retold in the forged wrinkles
of my own.
Can the morning really bring new birth?
That rises high upon the sky,
To sit and rest,
On a wrinkle, genuine,
A wrinkle owned
By one, but made for all.

*Claire Thomas*

# THROUGH THE EYES OF A CHILD
*(Dedicated to Jade Kirsty)*

I watched her knelt upon the ground,
Head bent, her look intense.
She didn't make a sound,
Her gaze one of wonder and awe.

She looked up into the flower,
Where a bee was busy at its work.
Discovering something new every hour,
Things I had long since forgot.
This tiny little child, her look of pure joy,
A nature so mild, as she turns back to her toy.

She cannot yet say much,
But she's discovering nature,
Its feel and its touch.
She's noticed flowers and birds,
and now there's a bee.
I find the joy of discovery,
has returned for me.

If I can guide her to love these things,
She'll gain happiness and joy,
From each bird that sings.

We can teach each other,
The old and the young,
To love one another,
And each living thing.

She's re-opened my eyes, to the wonder of life.
I forget all the sighs, about trouble and strife.
Through her eyes I see and notice each thing,
Beauty surrounds me, in each and everything.

She is my best friend, and she is not yet two.
Through her, I'm reliving my childhood,
And seeing things anew.

*Hilary Ann Torrens*

# MY DEAREST FRIEND

I could never list,
Every single thing,
I love about you
But here are just a few.

I love how you know
Exactly what's wrong
Before I even say,
What the problem is today.

I love how you hear,
The unspoken words
And we always *know*
Without us saying so.

I love how we share,
Every wildest dream,
And the things we fear,
Even though they're so weird.

And I love the fact
That when others change
And their friendship ends
You're still my dearest friend.

*Tara-Louise Huddless*

# A LOVING HAND

Husband dear come walk with me,
Come take me by the hand.
For life can be a rugged path
And not just what we planned.

December was our wedding day,
With fog and freezing ice,
The wedding bells they did forget
And no-one threw the rice.

But the vows we made in that small church,
They were made for life.
For we have been so happy,
Since we've been man and wife.

The children came a girl and boy,
Who then became our pride and joy.
Our lives they filled through night and day,
Till they had grown too old to play.

Their lives now filled with work and friends,
Their needs a different kind.
Now even more I need your hand,
To carry out the things we've planned.

*Elizabeth J Homes*

# MUM'S THE WORD

I'm you,
Yet I'm not,
I'm the you,
That you forgot.

You are me,
But not yet,
I'll be you soon,
And me I'll forget.

We'll change roles,
And for you I will care,
I'll use all you taught me,
And drive you spare.

You who are my friend,
My buddy, my chum,
I'm me because,
You're my Mum!

*Emma Legouix*

## UNSPOKEN WORDS

What's in my heart, in my mind, I find so hard to say,
As I awake - before I sleep - I search to find a way
To express my love, my feelings, they will never fade,
Life for me, its meaning - only you alone have made.
The joy, the warmth I feel whenever you are near,
You are my inspiration and forever, so very dear.
You give me strength and courage, to face what lies ahead,
We do not have to speak, for our unspoken words are said.
You say you do so little - loving me - you do so much,
A smile - that special look - I love your gentle touch.
One day those unspoken words, will be spoken and evolve,
Always my thoughts, my dreams, around you will revolve.

*Irene J Mooney*

## MY FRIEND

She told her tale
and sorrow cracked her voice;
cracked her face.
And though she clenched it fast
the pain squeezed out.

Weakly I put flesh on the bones
hardly understanding a bare ghost.
Yet, through years of strain;
the years of pain;
buffeted by unending
uncontrollable storms piled one upon another,
she blames herself
for decisions forced to make.

Her mind wracked with pain
her body too
yet I see power within her
refined through all this.
And all she could say was -
'Why does God
load us with such sorrows?'

Yet what I see; yet what she is
and what she lives
her vibrancy, her understanding
are the plant
that was nurtured by this horror.

*Marian J Lovelace Knight*

# MY BROTHER

Dear Steve, I know it's an honour,
To write this poem for you,
I know I'm very lucky,
To have a brother like you.

Your modesty, it must be said,
Has always been quite high,
You often blow your trumpet,
And you're certainly not shy.

Your humour's in a class of its own,
So dry and full of wit,
You always get your 'digs' in,
And they often hurt a bit.

Yet underneath that 'macho-image',
You're always trying to sell,
You can be sentimental,
Although you hide it well.

Remember Steve, as kids,
When told to give me a kiss,
You always screwed your face up,
It was a case of hit and miss.

But now you've reached your manhood,
The odd kiss I get I know,
Is the nearest sign of affection,
You are ever likely to show.

You say you are the best looking one,
Well that's not strictly true,
For I've got hair on top of my head,
Not very wide parting like you.

Jokes apart though, we've happy memories,
As we've grown up side by side,
I know the things you do not say,
That are buried deep inside.

So when 'Bradfords' is a dynasty,
And you've risen to fortune and fame,
When everyone wants to know you,
And pressure's the name of the game.

I'll be here just like always,
As this poem here will tell,
Remember it's written for you alone,
From me, your sister Michele.

*Michele Bescoby*

## FAMILY

Our family stands like a stout oak tree
Parental love giving rooted stability;
Siblings branching out into the world
Individual characteristics unfurled
Through life's seasons
Yet each retaining a family trait;
A love that though we don't demonstrate
Is there nonetheless binding us as one.

*Julia Cutting*

# LOVE'S EMBERS

The seasons change, the colours turn,
I see you as the man you were,
The uncut youth with much to learn,
Became a man but lost much more,
A crippled soul with emotional burn.

We loved and lost some time ago,
The rain beats down, the waters run,
I see you walk away, I feel the blow,
Our dreams are dust, the deed is done,
I don't need you now, that you know.

The snow comes down, pure and white,
The coldness cloaks all thoughts of love,
Despair and sadness is my right,
I see the stars and moon above,
Guide my thought in the cool, dark night.

Daffodils shake their yellow dresses,
I feel the sun's rays warm my skin,
The glow of day soothes and caresses,
My aching heart needs life to begin,
A new love comes, with joy it blesses.

The seasons change, the colours turn,
I see you as the man you are,
With finished youth, yet much to learn,
You're older now, we've come too far,
And reached the point of no return.

*Patricia A Tobin*

## OUR CHILDREN

To appreciate the beauty of a young child's face
With innocence shining in bonnets of lace
The delicate skin tones, so smooth and so fresh
The result of a miracle borne of the flesh
To hear a child cry, while annoying at times
Is something to cherish, like bells when they chime
Tiny fingers and toes, a nail on each one
So special to see on a daughter or son
For they grow up so quickly surpassing their mums
Enchanting their dads and asking them sums
Unless you are watching from when they can crawl
They'll be leaving the nest before they've grown tall
And those missing years you're unable to have
Will have passed you in no time, too late for the laughs
So hold on to each moment, so precious, so fine
Those threads will be broken at their marrying time.

*Kevin Murphy*

# IF

If I could love you more than I do.
I still would not be holding you.
The only way that could be,
Is if you could give your love to me.

If you ever feel lonely,
If you ever need somebody to hold.
When nights are long and cold.
If you could love me like I love you.
I could never be untrue.

If I could hold you close to me.
It would make me feel happy.
If I could take you for my wife.
I would love you for the rest of my life.

If you give me a chance.
I would never give another a second glance.
I would love you my whole life through.
If you let me give you love to you.

*Jason Foulkes*

## OCEANS APART

'Twas thy love I found cross thee ocean.
Brazil thy land captured me.
For thy heart it was enlightened.
Of a special place to see.
White sands and tropical sea beds.
I meet with thy destiny.
Thy heavenly moonlight settings.
Thy grace thy skies heavenly.
So noble and high in their splendour.
Each palm captured beauty to be,
God's gift and languages different.
And yet all in sweet harmony.
Thy music fun and laughter.
We sway to rhythm and slick.
Thy culture unique in its radical form.
And thy natives fantastic.

*Delline Docherty*

# THE CREEP

I know a guy,
I once adored.
But now he's changed,
And I feel no more.
He's selfish now,
He doesn't care.
I feel low
And I've bleached my hair.
He looks pretty moody
And passes me by.
Acts cool and calm,
But I know it's a lie.
He's got someone else,
He doesn't hide the fact.
He's not best known,
For sensitivity and tact.
When I see them together
I really could weep.
He used to be my boyfriend,
Now he's just the creep.

*Laura Cation*

## MUM

You mean so much to me mum you know,
and so much love you always show.
I always feel safe when I know you're there,
and happiness and love we always share.
There's no spite in you, there's only good,
and you always behave like a good mother should.
You give your opinions when I feel I don't need them,
I pretend not to listen, though often I heed them.
We both know we love each other very much,
Though we don't go round saying it as such.
But we show each other in different ways,
We spend time together and go out for days.
I know one day we will have to part,
And this is when I'll break my heart.
My life will no longer seem worthwhile,
Without my mum to make me smile.
So mum, I dedicate this poem to you,
You're special, you're wonderful and
      Mum,
          I love you.

*Helen Mousley*

# REFLECTIONS

I reflect upon a love long past
my heart filled with regret.
'If only this, if only that'
I might still have had thee yet.
Many summers since,
how long ago it seems,
yet how still across this span of time
you do haunt me in my dreams.
I never guessed, until too late,
how much you meant to me.
'Tis cruel fate
to discover that love now lost,
to know now it cannot be.
I hope that in a life hereafter
our paths will once more cross.
Until then, my darling Sharon
my heart must bear your loss.
Meantime, it is my hope
that through life you find success,
and may Cupid's arrow
find its mark
to bring you happiness.

*Carl H Simmons*

# ONE SWEET DAY

Friendship you'll find comes in lots of forms
When one sweet day into your life it storms
Never knowing the beginning or reaching the end
Once you've found that one very special friend

Lots of friends may pass by your way
But never like our one sweet day
Happiness created just for us two
Specially meant for me and you

Do you remember our moments together?
We knew, this time it would be forever
Thinking one sweet day we'll have to be
Holding each other close you and me

I'm sure one sweet day we'll find
Many happy memories come to mind
Open your eyes I'm always here
To tell you that I love you dear.

*M E Kirkman*

# THE FAMILY

We need each other day by day
As life is hard to take
When no-one else is there to say
'Hello' when you awake.

Sometimes a family is a bind;
They seem to interfere
With what we really have in mind,
And often cause a tear.

But when life gives us a hard knock,
And all seems lost to view,
'Tis then the family is the rock
That takes the strain for you.

Don't wait until it is too late
To tell them that you care.
Beware - don't leave it all to fate,
Or no-one may be there.

*Joan Picton*

## ODE TO GORDON WILSON

And now Gordon Wilson you are gone
Such beautiful and sad memories live on
On that sad Enniskillen day
When your lovely Marie was taken away
As she lay in the rubble she had to let you know
How she loved you so
'Daddy I love you so very much'
These are the words she said as she tried to clutch
your hand.
Than out of that terrible day
I just don't know how you could say
'I forgive them'

Like a beacon you shone to light the darkest night
Like a vision of hope for all that is right
Like a symbol of love and forgiveness too
Who can we now look to?
Is there anyone left in this island of ours
Who has such evangelic powers?
Who could talk to foe and friend the same
And try not to put the blame?
So from where you are now
Don't forsake us somehow
You know we need a guiding hand
To bring all people together in this land

*Vera McKeown*

# TO NELLA

A silver sapling,
wind-tossed blown through
frozen winter frost-bitter cold,
thawed and boldly laughed and danced
in summer sun
then stood to brave another winter:
all the winters, all the springs,
growing firm, resilient,
strong, adaptable,
roots embedded steadfast deep
leaves reaching wide and generous out
giving shelter, support and shade
or cheer in dappled pools of sun,
pointing to the wide, wide sky
in ever-encouraging Faith.

Then a new shoot arose
with the hope of spring:
in your arms you hold
your Grandson.
Cradled in the strength of years,
the melting of winter snows
and the gentle soft
kiss of the sun,
he sleeps peacefully.

*Karen Bayly*

# THE CIRCLE OF DESIRE

Sapphires sparkle in my sky
As I look out from my mind's eye

Golden lights dance in my head
As I lay dreaming in my bed

Unknown time and unknown place
The smile that forms across my face

The tingle running down my spine
As my thoughts mingle and entwine

The self-satisfaction of my desire
By the dancing flames of our passionate fire

A numbness creeps across my soul
As my emotions extract their toll

My body is weak, there's no more to give
But now more than ever I have desire to live

*Tom Sawyer*

# DAD

When I was young I remember my Dad,
we used to pick peas, and life wasn't so bad.

But then he went away, and the tension increased,
until divorce came along, and still there was no peace.

The visits were strained, my face, my undoing,
how could I know it caused pain renewing.

I hated my new life, and missed Dad so much,
I looked like my Mum, he couldn't reach out and touch.

So for nearly twenty years we never made a truce,
which would have released the love, and let the feelings loose.

Then you moved to the Island, and at last we made friends,
then the bitterness was laid to rest, and we made amends.

When you needed me most I was there,
and then all the family came, the vigil and pain to share.

Through death you reunited all your children in love,
then you left for your place in heaven above.

*Doreen Britton*

# A WORK OF ART

A child is born, we all rejoice
and shout hooray, hooray,
but as he grows a silence falls
as we hear someone say . . .
'There's something 'wrong',
he isn't 'right',
whatever can it be?
He appears to be quite 'normal'
but he's not like you or me'

Why can't we call him 'normal',
what other word is apt
to describe this little person?
of course . . .
he's handicapped!

He won't see life the way we do
and he may never understand,
he'll need us all to be there
to lend a helping hand.
He'll bring much love and happiness
to people near and far,
he'll make us question why we're here
and who we really are.
He'll give us everything he's got
with trusting open arms
and all he'll ever ask of us is that
we shield him from life's harms.

So if you see a child like this
don't turn and walk away,
stop and have a chat with him
he'll brighten up your day.

For who are we to take this child
and set him far apart.
He may not be like the rest of us
but he's a *work of art* . . .

*Dany Sherlock*

# THE FAMILY

What makes a family? I ask
That answer can be such a task.
Do we need both a mum and dad
For every lass and every lad?

Divorce is normal so we're told.
One parent less to hug and hold!
The children grow up without dad.
Do they now miss what they once had?

Work now dictates that dad's away,
And mum is left, all work no play.
The children grow up without dad.
Do they miss what they briefly had?

Mum's out at work, she needs her space.
She's tired and tense, life's such a race.
One day she finds another dad,
But he's not like the one we had!

We've got new sisters and a brother,
They've even got a new stepmother,
We liked the life that we once had;
The one we had with our dad.

We move away to look for work.
We need an income, mustn't shirk.
We leave behind gran and grandad,
There's tears and fears and all are sad.

We're grown up now. What is in store?
Family life! No there's much more.
Goodbye to pain, we'll just be glad.
We won't live life like mum and dad.
But what we'll put there in its place
Will be the problem we must face.

*Catherine Craft*

# THE THREE RICHARDS

Three Richards by chance
spanning such years and places
my different friends.

By the River Mole
Richard and I sat restful
talking of young love
shared cricket and thoughts of dawn
surprised at the swan's night dance.

Quietly he came
little Richard in the dusk
my dog greeted him
small Nigerian watchman
ever making safe the home.

There little Richard
in his cluttered Tokyo shop
sitting by the till
an aged war veteran
when I left he clutched my hand

Three Richards through time
across seasons, continents
universal friends.

*A P Graham*

## BUT HE WAS FAMILY

But he was family
Forgiven for the misdemeanours
Oh so many times.
Black sheep, adventurer,
Brave, daring, inveigling -
Those clever lines
We fell for, curling round
And weaving subtle spells
In our ordinary minds.

We loved the prodigal
More, because he made life uncertain, different, exciting
And drew us with him
On his rollercoaster journey
Onward, somehow inviting
Us to share the heights and hollows
Without quite censuring or joining.
Our love needed no requiting.

Now there is an empty silence
As the family gathers
Listening to a false homily.
His presence hugely absent,
Each individual's memories so varied
Of an errant whim or fancy
But none calls him rogue or villain -
Just remembers son, brother, lover,
You see, he was family.

*Jeffa Kay*

# A MEASURED WORTH

Mum
a simple word
of letters three
Priceless
a description
your value to me
Love
Lavished
without a thought
Life
given, shared
lessons taught
Supportive
a lending hand
the mother's creed
Friend
a comfort
in your hour of need
Valuable
a treasure
appreciated in ever way
Loved
with all our heart
more than words can say

*Chris Birkitt*

## NICOLA

Our darling little granddaughter,
A child so full of love,
Was sent to us one sunny day,
A gift from God above.
She is a little angel,
A child we all adore,
So full of fun and mischief,
We couldn't ask for more.
She sits upon my knee,
And plants a kiss upon my cheek,
A tender touch of innocence,
A love that's so unique.
Her eyes so full of love and trust,
A cheeky grin as well,
The extra special feeling
Of love we have for her.
Our darling little granddaughter,
Baby Nicola.

*S M Hunt*

# THE TROUBLE WITH JANE

Poor old Jane she's at it again
The way she behaves is a terrible shame
She's in love with Simon
She's in love with Paul
And she ends up committed to no-one at all
She complains that her life is empty and shallow
What can she expect when her actions are callow?
Each morning she's anxious - what will she wear?
And what in the world will she do with her hair?
She spends so much time on presentation
It's her only form of self-elevation
But it's superficial and goes only so far
Like the day she tried to buy a new car
She couldn't decide on the colour or make
And she flirted with salesmen, now that's a mistake
For she ended up buying no car at all
Then found herself dealing with ardent phone calls!
And then there's the question of what she should eat
Vegetarian, herbs, carbohydrate or meat?
And where should she go for her holiday this year?
Like the rest of her life - it's not very clear
Poor Jane has been a conundrum for years
It's pained her chums and brought her many tears
Like the shipwrecked sailor who did nothing at all
Poor Jane has her back firmly nailed to the wall!

*Julia Wallis-Bradford*

# HURT

I remember when you were my best friend; one to care
and compromise, understand, and love; one to share,
and be with , but no more.

So many years we have behind us, but now you go your
own way, leaving me to cope, and try to comprehend,

Shattered pieces everywhere, I pick them up, they fall
through air. What have I done, for you to say, 'I want
no more, I do not care'?

Awkward questions, no more time, move on they say, but
do they care?
Course not; having fun; going out together; forgotten me,
I may as well fly through air, since you fail to notice
separate paths; alone am I.

I used to feel so much for you, a great respect and
honoured love; but now, most gone, can never be replaced,
for you have said, 'There's nothing more to say.'
I cried till day was past, but you were gone, walked
through the door, no second word, hesitations do not work;
I tried. Alone am I.

Empty room, the four walls stare, your shadow left behind;
your heart still there . . . to grasp at straws, a foolish
fool, nothing to bear, but lonely air.

To be seated at the window sill, and see all down below,
I wonder if you're really there. Anonymous face, a
carefree mind, an empty heart is numb to bear.

Encased walls surround me now, barriers to myself, and I.
Leave it out, I still do care, but I hurt so much, I
need to be aware that no more hurt can bear me now,
forever more, immortalised am I.
Self-defence, it's hard to do, soft inside, a hardened
shell. You cracked it hard, rocked back and forth,
exposed inside, you've had your mirth.

---

I fail to understand what I've done so wrong, broken
eggshells, I walk on.
Tread carefully now, for you've hurt enough, you want this
now, but not before, what did I do, for you to call me
wrong? To walk away, when I was not strong.
Cried out am I, and empty core, my hurt still aches,
my eyes are tired. I still love you. I still want you.
Don't leave me now, or I will die. Hurt.

*Fiona E E Pearce*

# THIS LOVE

This love
Is one part
Of the oddest equation
Somehow its greatness
Reduces the other
Its constant avowal
Controls the loved
And it can
Without warning
Fly off at a tangent
Ascertaining its proof
With tortured logic
And explosive endearments
At the slightest stirring

While the other
Is seeking
An effective formula
To promote sensitivity
A little humility
(And maybe a tear)

Is there a recipe
For calm equanimity?
Can anyone help her
To square the circle?
If so, will you rush
Before this loved one
Gets loved
To point nought recurring?

*Edith Crompton*

## SELF

Sons they moan
and daughters nag,
husbands whine
life's such a drag,
each day brings more
crisis, shocks and worries too,
no straight path
to adhere to,
we walk alone
so out of touch,
with ourselves
we could have so much,
so find yourself
your truth is there,
look into yourself
become more aware,
to know yourself
and understand too,
would help with all
life puts you through.

*Tricia Morgan*

# SLOW TO LEARN

I miss the late-night story
That at eased me into sleep;
The man who knelt beside me,
To help me count the sheep.
I miss his morning welcome
At the start of each new day,
As I've missed him without failure
Since that day he went away.
How long childhood seemed to last
Through this young innocent's eyes.
A world where nothing alters,
And only the baddie dies.
A child , forever a child,
Both parents there to turn to.
Permanence never questioned;
You'd always help me through.
But those years slid past unnoticed,
And I didn't detect, or foresee,
That awful day when death took its shape,
And tore you away from me.
No time to make the transition;
To grow up, to prepare for the worst.
Just the rest of my life to figure out
Why I had been so cursed.

*Bryan Davies*

# FRIENDS
*(For Molly)*

Fair-weather, grasping, greedy, possessive,
Oh yes, so-called friends can be all these and more.
Love you in good times, and leave when you're drowning . . .
Those sorts of friends I could count by the score.

But those you can talk to and come when you're troubled,
Who will not judge when your secret's laid bare,
Who will stand by your side when they'll lose reputation,
Who'll not be afraid to see that fair's fair.

Who will find place for you when all else is failing,
Never demand till you're able to stand . . .
Those are the friends that are gold in the furnace,
Friends you can count on, on less than one hand.

*Sr Elizabeth Morris*

# FOOTPRINTS IN THE SAND

Turning, he noticed the funny little mark
of her heel in the sand.
Let's pretend we're lost said he
and follow the trail back.

Soon the track was lost.
They paused and remembered
they had veered to the right
avoiding the spray of the swimming dog.

Back on course they continued
towards the car and away
for the usual satisfying drink.
Somehow that evening it wasn't enough.

He wanted that something her soul wouldn't give.
Harsh words annihilated the friendship.
And the footprints that meant so much
were washed away by the tidal foam.

*Roisin Christie*

# LOOKING BACK

I came to this house with oh such joy:
Full of hope that time employ.
My family of three so young and bright.
After a while number four arrived.
Days of nappies, hard work, but pleasure.
These days I loved beyond all measure.
Seeing them grow into fine adulthood
Makes one feel as proud, as one could.
Now we have a new generation on whom we love
to devote our attention.
The house has seen a few little changes
But the family home is still a firm favourite.
Many years on, and here I sit, looking into the garden
Which, once was a football pitch, cycle track,
home-made slides, and tents.
Now it looks so quiet and still, but lovely to look onto.
So many memories, and I must say too:
I now partake in activities I once did do.

*Maisie Tompkins*

# FORGIVE ME FATHER

Forgive me, I was just a child,
for the hurt I caused,
and running wild.
For the bad things I have said and done,
the pain I caused
both you and Mum,
the lack of understanding why,
the words I spoke
would make you cry.

Forgive me now that I am grown,
with air and grace, a smile, I've shown,
a love that grew with years and light,
the teachings that, you thought were right.
A prickly thorn, now blooms a rose,
in place of hate, new words I've chose
before it's too late, to say to you:
I'd like to say . . .
that *I love you.*

*Amanda Southern*

## MUM

Mum I love you is the first and most
Important thing,
But to follow this as well a thank you I
Will bring,
You have made my years so happy and
Always been there,
You filled me with your love and a lot
Of gentle care,
You give me encouragement for which I
Am very grateful,
You've always been patient and stood by my
Every call,
And Mum I'll always be there as you
Have been for me,
And together we will live in peace for
All eternity.

*Sam J Shulver*

# MY KIND OF MAN

A man so dear, and kind
Has been married to me for thirty-four years.
For this a medal he deserves:
A short fuse of a temper, is a big fault of mine.
While he keeps so calm, and smiles, and smiles.
When each one of our four children arrived,
A very proud man stood by my side
He worked very hard, to build us a good home,
And took us on holidays, around Great Britain, and abroad.
We had our ups, and downs, as all couples do.
But with his great strength, he pulled us through.
Now retirement he has reached.
But he has no time to sit, and sleep.
He is as busy as can be, doing the jobs he promised me.
Then there's gold he wants to play,
And, maybe bowls another day.
But still he says, he is happy to be,
All alone with only me.
What a lucky lady me, to have a husband just like he.

*Dorothy Conway Trilk*

# FULL CIRCLE

Friends
Joyfully strolling
Holding hands
Skipping little girl
Questioning
Clouds sky
Trees flowers
Trustfully confident
Mother knows all
Good companions

Enemies
Teenage tumult
Traumas tantrums
Peace shattering
Screaming rages
Angry eyes
Ferocious faces
Tearful sobbing
Behind locked doors
Separation

Reconciliation
Repentance
Absolution
Apprehensive approaches
Friendship renewed
Hesitant hugs
Occasional kisses
Caring sharing
Walking arm in arm
Companions again

*Ann Sempers*

# FACES

An empty world full of faces,
All going different places,
Caring for themselves is what most of them do
It is hard to acquire a companion that is generally true.
A true friend is difficult to find,
The genuine compassionate caring kind.
We are all striving for our own recognition and a place to belong,
Life's everyday toils can make us all weak or strong,
Some are in the fast lane hurrying life away,
Others don't know what they'll do the next day
Each and every one out for their own
Their old school chums have all been outgrown,
Few stop to think that their life ticks on,
Few stop to care where old friends have gone,
The old lady sits alone with her bag on her knee,
No-one stops or cares who she might be,
A man leans against the train station wall,
Does anyone care if he is Peter or Paul?
It's an empty life full of careless faces,
Where people hurry to different places.

*Nicola Jayne Richardson*

# VOICE OF THE ABUSED CHILD

I am alone.
Invisible, silent.
A gliding, vigilant shadow.
Missing nothing.
Unseen, touching nothing.
Watch me as I bleed,
Dying, shrinking,
Little by little.
Detached, protected,
By the wall I've
Built around me.
Shrouded in secrecy,
Sharing nothing -
What have I to give?
Not wanting to be hurt.
Silently screaming
Desperate eyes imploring,
See what *they* have
Done to *me*.

*Beverley Christian*

## MY FAMILY

If I could pick out a family
I'd always choose my own
Because my family are so precious
And without them I'd be alone.

I'd choose a mother just like mine
Someone helpful, caring and there
My father I wouldn't change
Because he's always here to care.

I'd never swap my sister
The arguments or the fun.
My dear brothers can stay
Without them I'd be glum.

My family are so special to me
As is everything they do
And if they ever left me
I know I would feel blue.

*Sharleen Slater*

# A FRIEND FOR LIFE

When we need them most
They are always there
To help us out
And show that they care

Family relationships
Don't always work out
Brothers and sisters
They argue and shout

We choose our friends
With the utmost care
Our deepest thoughts
With them we share

We sail along on life's stormy sea
Not every day is calm
It's always so very comforting
To feel a supporting arm

In our journey through life
From beginning to end
The most constant thing
Is the love of a friend

*Margaret Robinson*

# FRIEND TO THE END

Oh how I wish the sun to rise
Within these glorious deep blue skies.
Then remember the warmth within your eyes,
How you spoke and loved so wise,
And then to know that you inspire,
All that glows within my heart's desire.

I feel within my heart Cupid's spears,
Then from my eyes flow silent tears,
Bringing back all my fears,
Of loving a man all these years,
I know now the time is near
For you to come home from afar my dear.

*Mags*

# TRANSGRESSION

Light of my life
husband, lover
happiness destroyer
where are you now?
Sleeping with her
the one I hate so much?

How could you do this?
Faithless deserter
why did it have to be?

Oh what a dreadful mess
I am so angry
lovelorn, lonely
will it ever end
this grief, this pain?

If there is a God
help me, help me
but God is long, long dead
and I am so alone

*Kate McDonnell*

# BUTTERCUP

A stroll; summer breezes wafting in from river breaths,
scatter-brained flies bumping to and fro.
The trees are shaking with invigoration,
the birds a call of delight on this midsummer eve.
Her hand in mine, waltzing through unspoilt pleasure,
unharnessed natural delights away from scornful eyes.
So illicit is this enjoyment I forget her hand in mine,
and drawn back suddenly by her curiosity on the ground.
A buttercup: prim and golden as the dying sun,
so effluently reflected upon our happy faces.
She plucks to smell, places under chin like a child,
reborn and grinning, enticing me into her world.
And I do.
All around us the buttercups are effulgent,
leaving me to ponder my ability to miss them all.
I turn towards the euphoric face staring back at me,
her hands a mass of yellow petals, but for one stem;
and to me extends this flower,
two tiny sunset leaves remaining.
Instinctively I pull them out, one by one.
He loves me not, . . . he loves me . . .
And indeed I do - and more -
surrounded by this meadow of sunset love.

*Andrew Tzionis*

# FAMILY

My poor mother -
Her brother was a war survivor,
Then died of that closespread disease.
My father was still mobilised
And I too young to understand
Her tortured mind.
But when my infant brother died
I shared her grief.
Two more sons were victims of the second war,
Shattering her life - my father's too.
I had to keep assistance in his work,
Disliking this, and live at home;
Then, when he died,
With sisters otherwise employed,
A home for two was left.
Then I collapsed in mental health,
Distressing so my mother more.
And then God saved my soul:
I married late; one sister took my place,
Though shortly motherless,
I fathered sons -
All three to take the place
Of brothers lost.
Soon I gave up the work not gladly mine,
To soothe the woes of children
I understood so well from past remembrances.
Retiring at the age I chose,
While sons enjoyed their choice
Of work and wife.
Mine, so much younger,
Assists to rear grandchildren close,
And cares for me with love untold,
As I survive the oldest male
In any generation of my kin.

*W I D Scott*

# FAMILY LOVE

My family and I like to be
quietly happy,
not talking about love,
but giving it.

Protrude little favours
that can often mean,
more than, I love you scenes.

Knowing when to stay away
give a cuddle, console,
or paracetamol.

Telling jokes Sunday lunch-time
listen to the whole story,
about a boring friend
they would be better off without it.

Giving confidence in tough beginnings
watching their first performance,
even though the role,
is only couple of words in all.

Talking love doesn't do for me
I take actions for signs of loving,
I could not say to my family
'I love you' without giggling.

I'll do anything for them
and they'll do it for me,
we don't need to say 'I love you'
because we know it.

*Silvia Kufner*

# LIFELONG FRIENDS

I meet friends in the market square
On weekdays when we're shopping there
Friends at church where I go to pray
And sing with them on each Sunday

Friends I had at childhood schools
Where we learned scholastic rules
I made friends when I started work
In the factory where we didn't shirk

My boyfriends were not numerous
I was so shy it wasn't humorous
My husband was a great friend who
Shared in tasks we had to do

My son is a quiet and caring man
Steps in to help others when he can
Sisters and brothers friends so strong
Gave a hand when things went wrong

Friendships cause us all to grow
In caring and sharing this we know
The two best friends I ever had
Were loving people my mum and dad

*E M Sheppard*

## MY GRANDSON

You are such a beautiful baby
A baby full of life
Born into this world today
Full of sorrow, full of strife

But I shall show you, grandson
All the wonders, all the magic
I shall protect you always
From times both hard and tragic

I shall help you understand
How to be considerate and tender
To grow up always caring
Loving any race and gender

I shall teach you to be strong
And you can teach me too
We can learn from one another
My grandson, I love you

*Christina R Maggs*

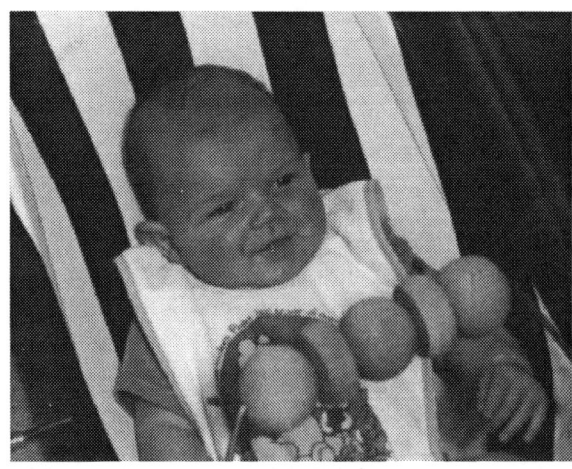

# MY FAMILY

My grandchildren bring me so much joy,
Three beautiful girls and two handsome boys.
What fun we have when they come to stay,
The years roll back through the games we play.
The sound of their laughter fills my heart
With love for this family, of which I am part.
From babyhood I've watched them grow,
Into the charming children they are now.
Each one an individual, so loved by me,
Tears fill my eyes when they sit upon my knee.
Their parents too, who with love and pride,
Work so hard, their footsteps to guide
Along the path of faith and trust,
Teaching them to be kind and just.
Last, but not least, my darling hubby,
Who, over the years, has grown slightly tubby.
My staunchest ally through sunshine and rain,
I would not hesitate to marry him again.
Thank you Lord for my family,
Please bless and keep them safe for me.

*Annelyn Jax*

# THE VIGIL

Come beloved, let us keep vigil together.
Time set apart to be at one with Me.
Come to Me to share your fears and desires.
Learn to escape from the bustle of life.
Be still and know, I am God,
I dwell in your inner sanctuary
And will be with you always.
Fear not for tomorrow and all its problems,
But live in the 'eternal now'.
As we watch together, our thoughts entwine
Great truths are revealed and you are given understanding.
My peace pervades your soul
And you are shown your place in My plan.
It is a time of quietness, deep love, recognition and joy.
You who share My vigil are blessed.
You who knock on My door, will find it open.
You who ask for petitions to be heard,
Will find them already granted.
You pray for help, I give it freely.
I the Creator of all, love My children
And rejoice that you dwell in My house.
Offer yourself as you are,
For in My eyes, your soul is perfection,
A true reflection of Me.

*Wilma Hogg*

## MEMORIES

Somehow you manage
to appear
upon the page I read.

You dare disrupt
reverie
as birds fly in to feed.

With stealth you knock
upon my door
at midnight or at dawn.

Unlikely times you
choose to visit,
when I am alone,

sleepless on a moonlit night
or as I lie awake at dawn.

*Ruby A Graham*

# LONELINESS

Do you know what it's like to be lonely and to be by yourself every day
In the daytime to have no-one to talk to, in the evening have nothing to say?
Every day starts the same as the last one, you wake up and you hear the birds sing
So you dress then you sit by the window and you hope that the doorbell will ring
No-one looks as they pass by your window not a greeting *hello* do you hear
Never a wave comes in your direction, no-one bothers for they think that you're queer
Loneliness is a terrible affliction, it can happen to the young and the old
You exist in a world that is silent, often hungry, seldom happy - always cold
The cold is because you are lonely no-one wraps you in the warmth of their love
You never have reason to be joyful, sometimes doubt there's a God up above
Maybe someone someday will take pity as they pass by the window on their way
They will stop, raise their hand in a greeting and say 'How are you, isn't it a nice day?'

*Pat Pritchard*

# IF I SHOULD FALL FROM YOUR FRIENDSHIP
*(For Helen)*

If I should fall from your friendship,
Then I will linger in the darkness of
An unfathomable Universe where,
I will feel lonelier than a fading star.
If I should fall from your friendship,
I will be sadder than the end of the world
And my sadness will last an eternity.
If I should fall from your friendship,
I will be trapped in a soulless body
Far, on an unmarked road of despair.
If I should fall from your friendship,
Darkness will descend, dreams will be no more.
If I should fall from your friendship,
This heart, I would tear out, for it would
Not be worth its beating, beating, no,
If I should fall from your friendship.

*Roman Suchyj*

## SUEZ ROAD CAMBRIDGE

When I was a child
I lived in a street
Where poverty reigned supreme.

Though poor materially
We were rich in spirit.

We shared the little we had
Borrowed, knowing we weren't expected to pay back.
So many cups of sugar
Passed over the garden fence,
Tea, milk, outgrown clothes, leftovers,
Nothing ever thrown away.

A knock on the party wall
Brought help and a sympathetic ear.
No need for social workers
No time for counsellors or such.

Nothing too much trouble
No-one left alone or forgotten.

This was a proud, strong community
We took care of our own.
Nursed each other when ill,
Collected money for flowers when bereaved
And closed the curtains in respect.

The community is broken now
Some died, children grown to maturity
Others moved away.
But it lives on in memory.

I was born into an area of social deprivation,
Labelled underprivileged
But I learned things that
Education can never teach
Nor money ever buy
Or begin to compensate for.

Riches of the spirit
This is wealth beyond compare.

*Janet Cullup*

## INFORMATION

We hope you have enjoyed reading this book - and that
you will continue to enjoy it in the coming years.
If you like reading and writing poetry drop us a line, or
give us a call, and we'll send you a free information pack.

Write to:
Poetry Now Information
1-2 Wainman Road
Woodston
Peterborough
PE2 7BU
(01733) 230746